Sachin Tendulkar

by

Andy Croft

Illustrated by Dylan Gibson

First published in 2011 in Great Britain by
Barrington Stoke Ltd
18 Walker St, Edinburgh, EH3 7LP

www.barringtonstoke.co.uk

ISBN: 978-1-84299-950-9

Printed in Great Britain by Bell & Bain Ltd

From the Author

Cricket is a funny game. If you don't know the rules, it just looks like a lot of people standing around in a field. Cricketers use funny words like silly mid-off and silly mid-on, googlies and beamers, dinks and daisy-cutters, ducks and donkey-drops.

Even the rules of cricket sound funny. Think about it. There are two sides, one is out and one is in. When all the players are out, the side that was out comes in. The side that was in then tries to get the other team out. When both sides have been out twice the game is over ...

But cricket can also be an amazing sport. Great players combine sport and art, sweat and grace, strength and beauty.

Sachin Tendulkar is one of the greatest players of all time. Here is his story.

Contents

Chapter 1

The Little Champion

The Indian cricketer Sachin Tendulkar is one of the greatest batsmen of all time.

He holds the record for scoring the most runs in both Test and One Day International cricket. He also holds the record for scoring the most centuries in Test and One Day

International cricket (a century is 100 runs). He is the only player to have scored 200 runs in one game in the history of One Day Internationals. He is the first player ever to score 50 centuries in international cricket.

He has played more Test matches than any other Indian cricketer. He holds the record (with Brian Lara) for hitting the fastest 10,000 runs in Test cricket. He is the only batsman to score over 3000 runs against the same team – and he has done it twice, against both Sri Lanka and Australia.

Tendulkar has millions of fans all over the world. In India his fans sometimes say, "cricket is my religion and Sachin is my God". The Australian bowler, Shane Warne, says Tendulkar is the best player he ever played against. Matthew Hayden once said, "I have seen God. He bats at number 4 for India."

He is the only modern player picked by the famous Australian cricketer Don Bradman for his all-time cricket team, *Bradman's Eleven*.

Tendulkar is a hero. He is a giant in the world of sport. But he is only 5 foot 4 inches tall. That's why his fans call him "the Little Champion" and "the Little Master".

Chapter 2

The Little Master

Sachin Tendulkar was born on the 24th of April 1973, in the Indian city of Bombay (now called Mumbai). He was the last of four children. His father was a poet. His mother worked in a bank.

Everyone in India is mad about cricket. Most of all in the city of Mumbai. Some of India's most famous cricketers have come from there.

When Sachin was little, his elder brother showed him how to play cricket. They used to play with other boys in the local park after school. He was more interested in playing cricket than in his lessons. At first he wanted to be a fast bowler. He was good. But he was an even better batsman.

He practised for hours in the nets, before and after school. His coach used to put a one-rupee coin on the top of the cricket stumps. Anyone who could bowl Tendulkar out could keep the coin. If no one could bowl him out, Tendulkar could keep it. He soon made a lot of money!

By the time he was 11 he was playing with much older boys in the school team. He also played for the Young Parsee Club. Then for the John Bright Club. He scored his first century when he was 12.

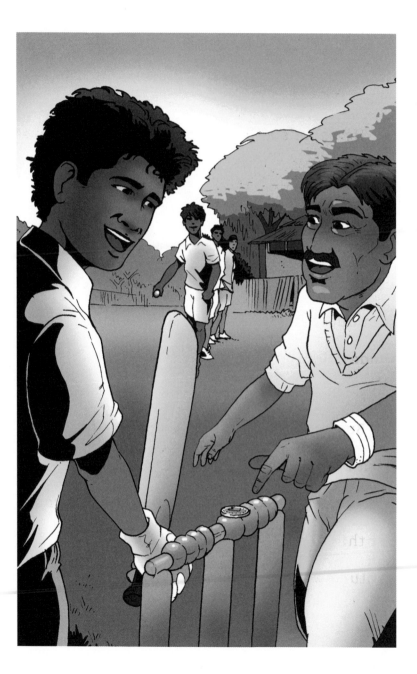

When he was 15 he scored over a 1000 runs for his school team in one season. He scored a century in every innings! In one game he scored 329 runs. He and Vinod Kambli (who also later played for India) scored 664 between them. It was a world record!

People were soon talking about the wonder boy from Mumbai. The Indian batting legend Sunil Gavaskar gave him a pair of his own cricket pads.

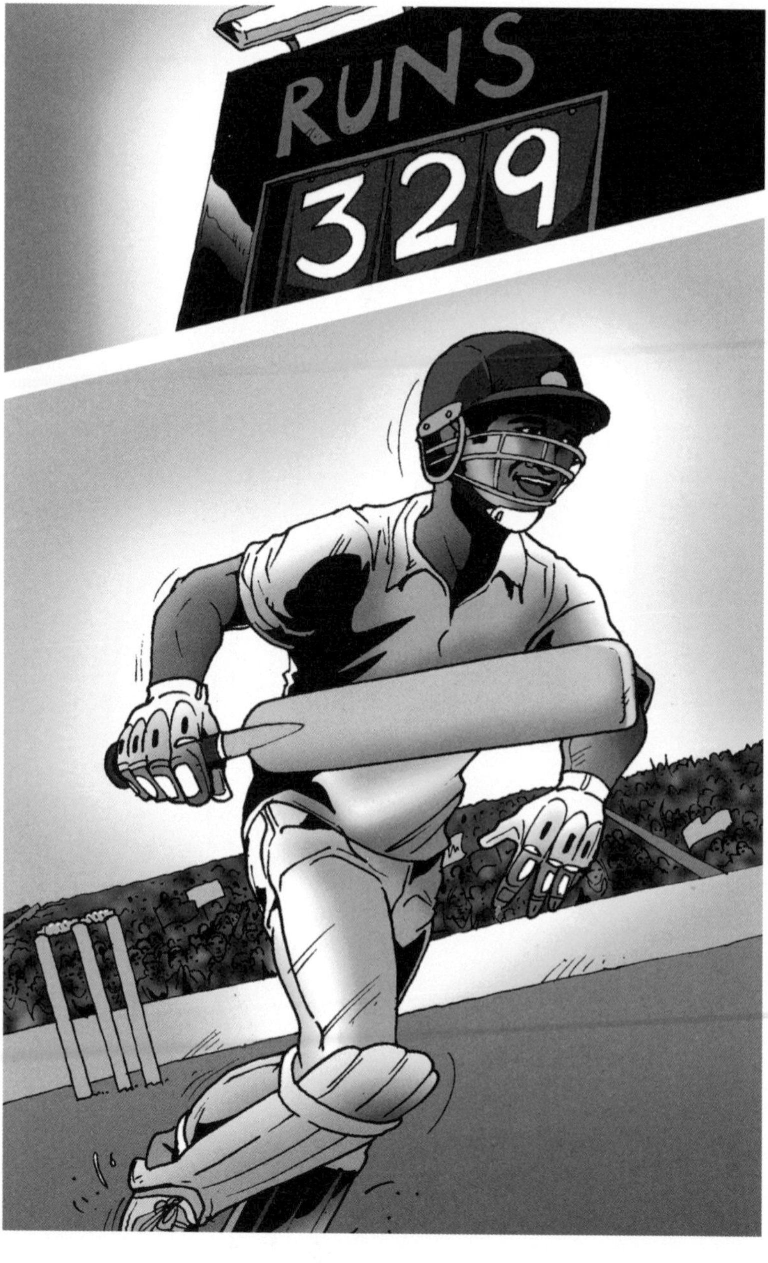
RUNS
329

Another cricketing legend was about to be born.

Chapter 3

The Bombay Bomber

Sachin Tendulkar played his first game for Bombay on 11 December 1988. It was against Gujarat. He scored 100 not out. This made him the youngest Indian player ever to score a century in his first professional game. Another record broken. And he was still only 15.

He scored another century in his first Deodhar and Duleep Trophy game. He made another in the Irani Trophy final. At the end of his first season he was Bombay's highest run-scorer.

At the end of that season he was selected to play for India on a tour of Pakistan. In November 1989, he became India's youngest ever Test cricketer, when he played against Pakistan. He made 15 runs before he was bowled out. In the final Test, he was hit on the nose by a bouncer, but he carried on playing with a bloody nose. At the end of the

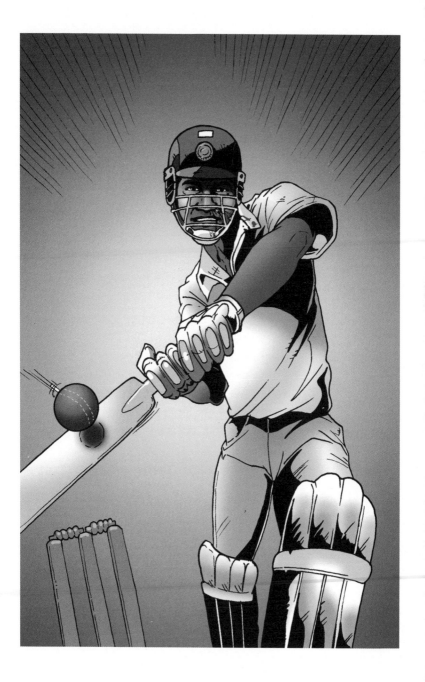

series he had scored 215 runs, at an average of 35 runs in every innings. Not bad for a 16-year-old. That's why they called him the Bombay Bomber.

Tendulkar was soon a regular in the Indian side. He scored 88 on a tour of New Zealand. Then in 1990, he became the second youngest cricketer ever to score a Test century when he made 119 runs against England at Old Trafford.

The following year he hit two centuries against Australia (148 in Sydney and 114 in

Perth). In 1994 he scored 179 against the West Indies. He scored his first One Day International century in 1994 against Australia.

In August 1996, Tendulkar was made captain of India. He was still only 23. He led India to the semi-finals of the 1996 Cricket World Cup. On the way, he hit two centuries and 523 runs to become the top scorer in the competition.

He hit three centuries in three innings against Australia in early 1998. In the 1999

Cricket World Cup he scored 140 against Kenya (off 101 balls).

Tenulkar was every bowler's nightmare. The simply could not get him out. But he was also every Indian cricket fan's greatest dream.

Chapter 4
Tendulkar

Tendulkar may be one of the greatest batsmen in the world, but he never stops practising. "Whatever level you reach, getting better never stops," he says. "You want to be on top of your game all the time and push yourself harder and harder. It's a great challenge."

He has perfect timing, a good eye and quick feet. He is powerful and brave. And he can use both hands. He writes with his left hand. But he plays cricket with his right hand. He even catches with his right hand. He has made over 100 Test catches for India.

He is also a brilliant bowler! He can bowl in lots of ways – medium pace, off-break, leg-break, leg-spin and off-spin. So far he has taken 44 Test wickets and 154 wickets in One Day Internationals. In fact, he is India's ninth all-time highest wicket-taker in One Day International games.

Against Australia in early 1998, he took 5 wickets in a One Day International game. Australia were in a very strong position at 203 for 3. But then Sachin Tendulkar came in to bowl. In 10 overs he took 5 wickets for just 32 runs.

In the ICC 1998 quarter-final in Bangladesh, he hit 141 runs – and then took 4 Australian wickets. On the final day of the Kolkata Test against Australia in 2001, he took the vital wickets of Hayden and Gilchrist.

Tendulkar is so good that his fans sometimes call him *Ten*dulkar, because he is worth ten men. He is more modest. "It's not about records," he once said. "It's all about loving the game and enjoying being out there in the middle ... but you've got to find a reason to go out there, and for me the reason is very clear. I play because I love the game."

Sachin Tendulkar believes that cricket should be played fairly. On India's tour of South Africa in 2001, he was punished for cleaning the ball. Indian fans were very angry. They knew that Tendulkar would

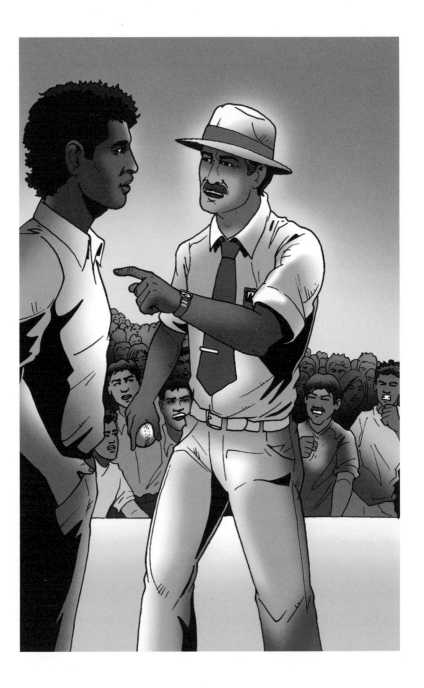

never cheat. For him, cricket is not about winning, but about playing the beautiful game.

"From the age of three I've loved this sport and I've never thought about scoring the most number of centuries or runs in international cricket. Everyone enjoys breaking records. I'm enjoying it too, but that is not the reason I play cricket."

Chapter 5
*End*ulkar?

Sachin Tendulkar started well in the 2002 series in the West Indies. In the first Test he hit 79 and 117. But in the next four innings he scored 0, 0, 8 and 0. India lost the series. The next year was even worse. His batting average was only 17.25.

When India toured Australia in 2003-4 Tendulkar was out for 0, 1, 37, 0 and 44. Although he hit 241 in the last Test of the series, a bad elbow kept him out of the Indian side for most of the year.

In the Test series in Pakistan in 2006, he was bowled out for just 26 in the second Test. When he was out for 1 in the third Test against England in Mumbai, the crowd started booing. They were booing their hero, Sachin Tendulkar.

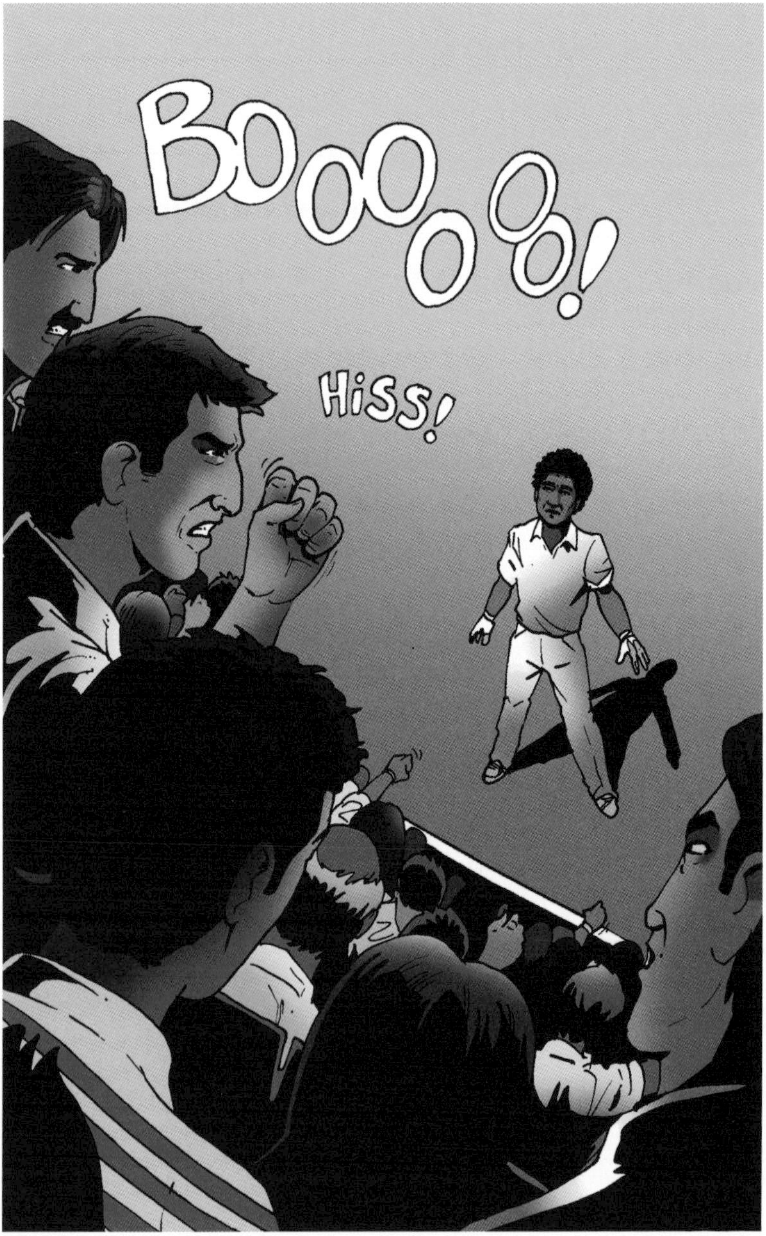
BOOOOOO!
HISS!

After an operation on his shoulder, he was back for the 2007 Cricket World Cup in the West Indies. But he only scored 7 against Bangladesh and 57 against Bermuda. He was out for a duck against Sri Lanka.

There was something wrong with Tendulkar's game. He was playing more slowly. His game was more defensive. He didn't hook or pull his shots like before. He even seemed nervous. In 2007, Tendulkar was out 7 times just short of a century (he was out 3 times when he was on 99). Against Sri Lanka in 2008, he only needed 177 runs to beat Brian Lara's record of 11,953 runs in Test cricket. But in 6 innings he scored a total of just 95 runs.

It looked for a while as if Tendulkar's amazing story was coming to an end. Some people joked that he ought to change his name from Tendulkar to Endulkar. Even his biggest fans thought it was time for Tendulkar to retire.

But the Little Master never gave up. He just trained harder than ever. "There comes a time when people will throw stones at you," he said, "but only you can turn those stones

into milestones."

Chapter 6
Master Blaster

By the beginning of 2008, the Master Blaster was back to his best.

In the Border-Gavaskar Trophy in Australia, Tendulkar was the leading scorer with 493 runs in four Tests. In the Test series between India, Sri Lanka and

Australia, he became the first batsman to hit 16,000 runs in One Day International cricket.

The next year against Australia he hit 13 and 49 in the first Test, then 88 in the second Test. This broke Brian Lara's record for Test runs. He also passed the 12,000 Test run mark. He made 50 in the third Test and 109 in the fourth.

He hit 103 not out against England in 2008. The next year he hit 163 and 160 against New Zealand.

In a seven-match One Day International series against Australia, Tendulkar became the first player ever to score 17,000 runs in One Day Internationals. In the fifth match he hit 175 off 141 balls.

He scored 100 against Sri Lanka in 2009-10. Against Bangladesh he made 105 not out in the first Test, and 143 in the second. In the 2010 series against South Africa, he hit 100 in the first Test and 106 in the second.

The second One Day International of the series was played in India.

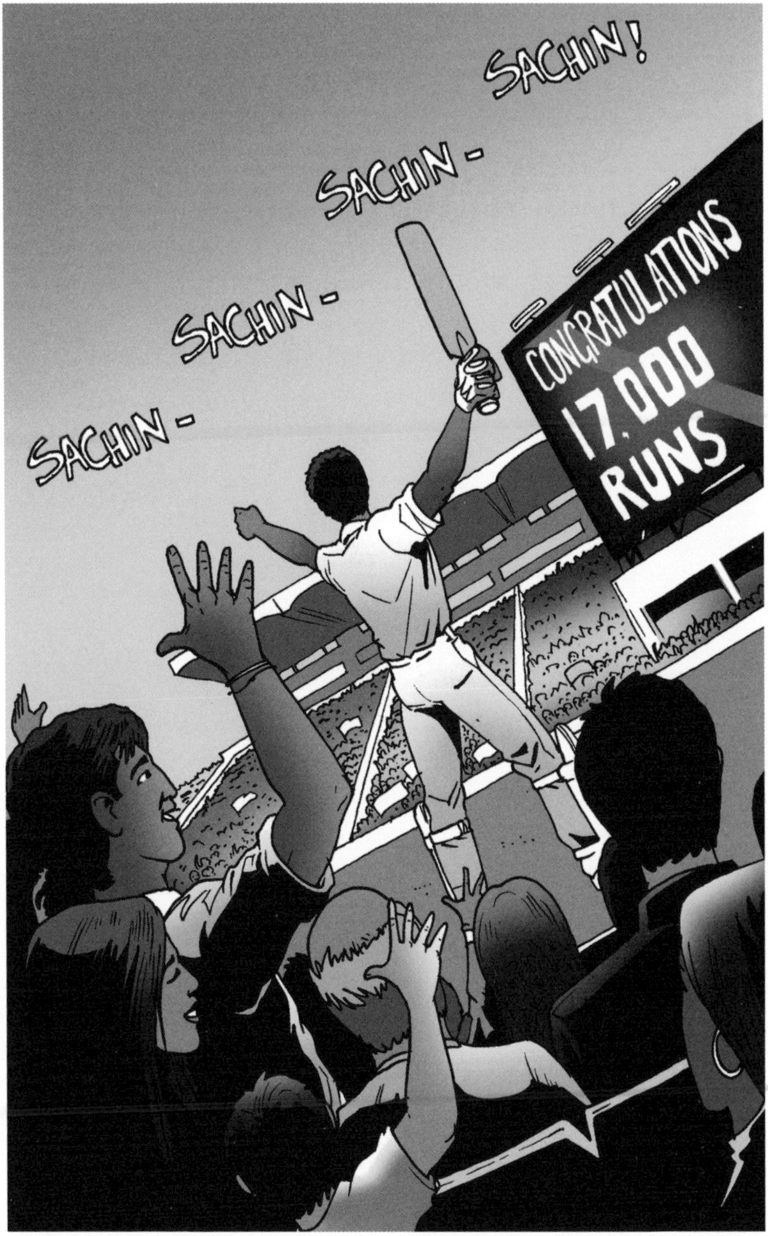
SACHIN - SACHIN - SACHIN - SACHIN!
CONGRATULATIONS
17,000
RUNS

Tendulkar was batting. It looked like he might beat the world record score of 194 in a One Day International (set by Pakistan's Saeed Anwar). But at the beginning of the last over he was still on 199. Only 6 balls left. Then Dhoni hit a quick single. Tendulkar was facing the bowler. Five balls to go. Could he do it? Or would nerves get in the way again?

Bang! He hit the next ball right through the gully. 200 not out! The Master Blaster was back.

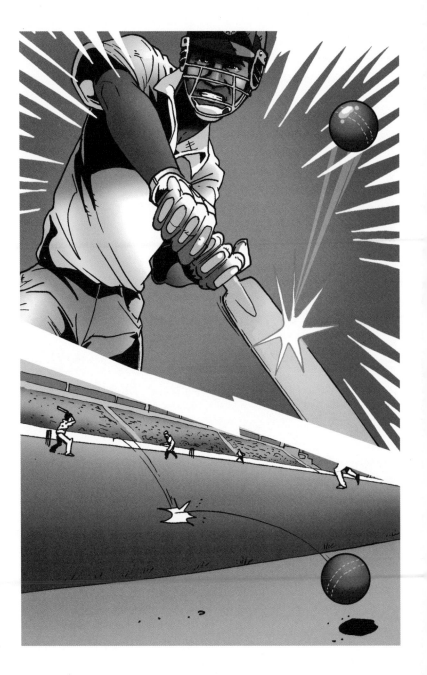

No one says that Tendulkar should retire these days. He may be 37, but there are still more records waiting to broken. Can he break the record for the most Test caps in the world? (He has 168 caps, just 2 behind Steve Waugh.) Will he be the first man to score a total of 100 centuries in international cricket? (At the moment he has 93 centuries.) Can he score a triple-century in a Test innings?

The next Cricket World Cup is in 2011. In India. In Mumbai. Tendulkar will be there. Anything is possible.

Chapter 7
Super Hero

Sachin Tendulkar still lives in Mumbai
with his family. His wife Anjali is a doctor.
They have two children. He doesn't like
people taking photos of his wife and children.
He is a very private man. He likes staying at
home and listening to music. He has

thousands of CDs. He is also learning to play the guitar.

But it is hard to live a normal life when you are the most famous person in India. He can only go out at night. If he goes out during the day he has to wear a wig. Sometimes he drives his Ferrari round the streets of the city late at night just to enjoy some peace and quiet.

He sponsors 200 poor children every year through a charity in Mumbai. He has just written a book about his life. He is using the

money to build a new school in Mumbai. The books cost £50,000 each!

When he is not playing cricket he likes playing tennis. His all-time favourite tennis player is John McEnroe.

Today, Sachin Tendulkar is the highest paid cricketer in the world. He earns 700 million rupees a year (£10 million). He is one of the richest men in India. He owns restaurants. His photo is used to sell cameras, trainers, cars, banks, tooth-paste, tyres, credit cards, motor-bikes, TVs, soft drinks, shoes and biscuits. You can see his smiling face on adverts all over India.

There is a wax statue of him in Madame Tussaud's in London. There is a Bollywood musical about his life. There is even a series of comic books, cartoons and games about a superhero who wears armour and carries a flaming cricket bat. His name? Master Blaster!

Chapter 8

10 Things You Probably Didn't Know About Sachin Tendulkar

1. His parents named him Sachin after the famous Indian singer Sachin Dev Burman.

2. At school he used to be in trouble for fighting.

3. He was the first batsman to be given out by the Third Umpire (by TV replay).

4. He is the only batsman to have made a century on his birthday (in 1998).

5. He is the only batsman to be out LBW (Leg Before Wicket) when the ball hit his helmet! (He bent down to avoid a bouncer).

6. He was the first overseas player to play for Yorkshire.

7. He is the only player to score a century in the first games he played in the Ranji, the Duleep and the Irani cups.

8. He always keeps an Indian flag inside his kit bag.

9. He always puts his left pads on first.

10. When he joined Twitter he had 80,000 followers in 24 hours.

Barrington Stoke would like to thank all its readers for commenting on the manuscript before publication and in particular:

James Ribbons
Anne Stockdale
Josh Thomson
Jonathan Tomlinson
Martin Walton
Karen Williams

Become a Consultant!

Would you like to be a consultant? Ask your parent, carer or teacher to contact us at the email address below – we'd love to hear from them! They can also find out more by visiting our website.

schools@barringtonstoke.co.uk
www.barringtonstoke.co.uk

**Lewis Hamilton
by
Andy Croft**

Lewis Hamilton is the first ever black Formula 1 champion.
How did he get from go-karts to global fame? Find out here!

**Sol Campbell
by
Andy Croft**

From racism to success.
From hard times to fast cars.
From school team to World Cup squad.

The true story of fame, fortune and a footballing superstar.

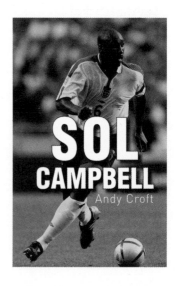

You can order these books directly from our website at
www.barringtonstoke.co.uk

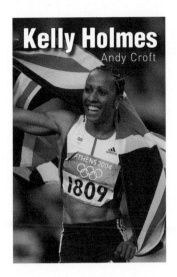
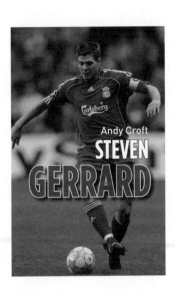